FINANCIAL FREEDOM: THE WEALTH BLUEPRINT

A Beginner's Guide to Personal Finance

Anna Jane

CONTENTS

Title Page
Introduction
#1: Why Money Matters   1
#2: Budgeting Like a Boss   4
#3: Debt—Friend or Foe?   8
#4: Saving Is the New Cool   12
#5: Getting Paid Like a Pro   16
#6: Investing Basics for Beginners   21
#7: Spending Wisely   25
#8: Adulting Essentials   29
Conclusion: You've Got This!   33
Bonus Section 1: Money Hacks Everyone Should Know   35
Bonus Section 2: Financial FAQs Answered   40

INTRODUCTION

"Adulting is hard enough—don't let money be one more thing to stress about."

Congratulations! If you're reading this, you're already ahead of most people. Why? Because you're taking the first step to understand something that impacts every aspect of life—money. Whether you're fresh out of high school, starting your first job, or just tired of feeling like your paycheck disappears too quickly, this book is for you.

Why This Matters

Let's be real: money touches almost everything. Want to travel the world? Money. Dreaming of your own apartment? Money. Even basic stuff like buying groceries or having a Netflix subscription requires you to manage your finances. Yet, so many of us are thrown into the adult world without any real knowledge about handling money.

Here's the thing: Money isn't about being rich. It's about being free. Free from stress about bills. Free to take opportunities when they come up. Free to live the life you want.

Imagine this: Two friends, Alex and Jordan, each make $2,000 a month.

- Alex spends every dollar and has nothing saved. When their car breaks down, Alex has to borrow money, which puts them deeper in debt.

- Jordan, on the other hand, sets aside $200 each month. When Jordan's car breaks down, they use their emergency fund and avoid the stress Alex is facing.

Same income, two very different outcomes. The only difference? Money management.

What You'll Learn

This book is designed to help you:

1. **Take Control**: Create a budget that actually works for you.
2. **Save Smart**: Build an emergency fund and save for the things you care about.
3. **Grow Your Money**: Understand the basics of investing and how it can work for you.
4. **Make Better Choices**: Spend mindfully without feeling guilty or broke.

But don't worry, we're not here to bore you with lectures or complicated financial jargon. Every chapter is packed with practical tips, fun examples, and simple steps you can actually follow.

Set a Goal

Before we dive into the nitty-gritty, take a moment to think about **why** you care about money.

- Do you want to save for a car?
- Pay off a loan?
- Stop worrying about unexpected expenses?

Write it down! Here's an example to get you started:

- **Goal**: Save $1,000 for a vacation by next summer.
- **Why It Matters**: I want to enjoy my trip without worrying about debt or feeling broke when I get back.

Having a clear goal makes learning about money feel more personal and meaningful.

By the time you finish this book, you'll:
- Know exactly where your money is going.
- Feel confident about saving and spending.
- Have a plan to start growing your wealth—no matter where you're starting.

Remember, you don't need to be perfect. Managing money is a skill, and like any skill, it gets better with practice. Let's get started!

#1: WHY MONEY MATTERS

Have you ever wanted to say "yes" to something without worrying about money? Maybe it's a road trip with friends, upgrading your phone, or grabbing your favourite coffee without guilt. Financial independence gives you the freedom to do those things—not just now but in the future too.

Here's an Example

Think about Sara, a college student with a part-time job. She manages her money well by saving a bit each month. When her friends plan a weekend trip, Sara doesn't think twice—she's been saving for moments like this. Compare that to her friend Mike, who's always short on cash and has to borrow money from others to join in.

Same life stage, different experiences. The difference? How they handle money.

Money as a Tool, Not a Goal

Here's the secret: Money isn't about having stacks of cash to show off. It's about what it allows you to do. Whether it's paying your bills, buying your dream car, or retiring early, money is the tool that gets you there.

Mindset Shift

Instead of thinking, *"I'm bad with money"* or *"I'll never have enough,"* flip the script to:

- "I'm learning to manage my money."

- "I can create a plan to reach my goals."

Remember, no one is born knowing how to manage money—it's a skill you can learn.

Why You Need to Care About Money Now

You might think, *"I'm young. I'll deal with money later."* But starting now—even with small amounts—gives you a huge advantage. Here's why:

- **Time is on your side**: Saving or investing a little now grows into a lot later because of compound interest (we'll explain this in Chapter 4).
- **Build habits early**: The earlier you develop good money habits, the easier it becomes to handle bigger financial decisions later.

Picture this:

- If you save $50 a month starting at age 20, you'll have over $60,000 by age 50 (assuming a modest 6% annual return).
- Wait until you're 30 to start, and you'll only have about $32,000.

The takeaway? Starting small now beats waiting to save "big" later.

Your Money Snapshot

Let's make this personal. Answer these questions:

1. How much money do you make each month? (This could include part-time jobs, allowances, side gigs, etc.)
2. How much do you spend? (Think bills, subscriptions, eating out, shopping.)
3. Do you save anything? If yes, how much?

Write your answers down. This snapshot will help you see where you are now and what you might want to change.

Quick Tip

Not sure where your money goes? Track it for one week. Write down every expense, from coffee to gas. The results might surprise you!

What's Coming Next

In this chapter, we talked about why money matters and how financial independence gives you freedom. Next, we'll dive into the basics of **budgeting**—a simple way to keep your money organized so you can save for what truly matters.

#2: BUDGETING LIKE A BOSS

Let's clear something up—budgeting isn't about saying "no" to everything fun. It's about having a plan for your money so you can say "yes" to the things that matter most. Think of a budget as a map for your money. Without one, it's easy to get lost.

Imagine you get $500 this month from your part-time job. Without a plan, it's easy to spend it all on random things like fast food, clothes, and Netflix. But when your car needs gas or you want to buy a concert ticket, you're out of cash. A budget helps you avoid these moments by giving every dollar a purpose.

The 50/30/20 Rule Simplified

A popular budgeting method is the **50/30/20 Rule**. Here's how it works:

1. **50% Needs**: Essentials like rent, groceries, utilities, transportation.
2. **30% Wants**: Fun stuff like eating out, streaming services, or shopping.
3. **20% Savings**: Emergency fund, debt repayment, or long-term savings.

Relatable Example

Let's say you earn $1,000 a month:

- **$500 (50%)** goes to needs (e.g., $300 for rent, $100 for groceries, $100 for gas).
- **$300 (30%)** goes to wants (e.g., $150 for shopping, $50 for Netflix and Spotify, $100 for fun nights out).

- **$200 (20%)** goes to savings.

Adjust these percentages if your situation is different, but the key is to always save something.

Tools to Make Budgeting Easy

You don't need fancy spreadsheets or hours of free time to budget. Here are some tools that make it simple:

- **Apps**: Try Mint, YNAB (You Need A Budget), or EveryDollar for automated tracking.
- **Envelope Method**: Use physical envelopes or digital categories to divide your money (great for cash users).
- **Spreadsheets**: A basic Google Sheet works wonders if you prefer a DIY approach.

Quick Tip

Set up alerts on your bank app to track spending or to notify you when your balance is low. It's an easy way to stay on top of things.

How to Create Your First Budget

Follow these steps to create a budget that works for you:

1. **Write Down Your Income**
   Include all sources: paycheck, allowance, side hustle income.

2. **List Your Expenses**
   Break them into two categories:
   - **Fixed Costs**: Rent, car payment, subscriptions (things that stay the same each month).
   - **Variable Costs**: Groceries, entertainment, gas (things that fluctuate).

3. **Subtract Expenses from Income**
   - Do you have money left over? Awesome!

Allocate it to savings or debt repayment.
- Are you spending more than you earn? Look for areas to cut back, like eating out or unused subscriptions.

4. **Set Savings Goals**
   - Short-term: Emergency fund, concert tickets, new shoes.
   - Long-term: A car, a trip, or investing.

Make Your Own Budget

Use this simple table to create your budget. Fill it out based on your current income and expenses.

Category	Amount
Income	$
Needs (50%)	$
Wants (30%)	$
Savings (20%)	$
Total Income - Expenses	$

Common Budgeting Mistakes to Avoid

1. **Underestimating Expenses**: Don't forget things like random coffee runs or birthday gifts.
2. **Not Adjusting for Life Changes**: Your budget should adapt when your income or expenses change.
3. **Cutting Too Much Fun**: If your budget feels like a punishment, you're less likely to stick to it.

What's Next

Now that you know how to budget like a boss, you're ready to tackle **debt** in Chapter 3. We'll talk about good vs. bad debt and how to keep it under control—without stressing out.

#3: DEBT—FRIEND OR FOE?

The Truth About Debt:
Debt isn't always a bad thing, but it can feel like a never-ending storm if you don't manage it wisely. The key is understanding the difference between **good debt** and **bad debt** so you can use it to your advantage instead of letting it hold you back.

Good Debt vs. Bad Debt

- **Good Debt**: This is money borrowed for something that grows in value or benefits your future. Think student loans (investing in education), mortgages (buying a home), or starting a business.
- **Bad Debt**: This is debt from things that lose value or don't help you build wealth. Think credit card balances from shopping sprees or payday loans with sky-high interest rates.

Example

- Borrowing $10,000 for college can lead to a better-paying job in the future. That's **good debt**.
- Borrowing $5,000 to buy a high-end gaming system? Fun, but financially, that's **bad debt**.

How Debt Works

Whenever you borrow money, you don't just pay back what you

borrowed—you pay **interest**, which is a fee for borrowing.

- **Low Interest (Good)**: Mortgages, student loans, and some personal loans.
- **High Interest (Bad)**: Credit cards and payday loans.

Think of interest as a "rental fee" for borrowing money. The longer you take to pay it back, the more you owe.

Quick Math

If you buy a $1,000 laptop on a credit card with 20% interest and only pay the minimum payment each month, you'll end up paying about $1,800 by the time you're done! That's like buying the same laptop twice.

How to Manage Debt Like a Pro

If you already have debt, don't panic. Here are steps to get control:

1. **Know What You Owe**
    - Make a list of all your debts: who you owe, how much, the interest rate, and the monthly payment.
2. **Prioritize Payments**
    - Use the **Snowball Method**: Pay off the smallest debt first for quick wins.
    - Or try the **Avalanche Method**: Pay off the debt with the highest interest rate first to save the most money.
3. **Set a Payment Plan**
    - Add debt payments to your budget (see Chapter 2).
    - Always pay at least the minimum payment to avoid penalties.

4. **Negotiate Your Rates**
   - Call your credit card company or lender and ask for a lower interest rate. You'd be surprised how often they say yes.

Avoiding the Debt Trap

To keep debt from piling up, follow these tips:

1. **Use Credit Cards Wisely**
   - Only charge what you can pay off in full each month.
   - Treat your credit limit as your budget cap, not extra money to spend.
2. **Emergency Funds First**
   - Save for emergencies (like car repairs or medical bills) so you don't rely on credit cards.
3. **Say No to Payday Loans**
   - These loans might seem convenient, but their high interest rates can trap you in a cycle of debt.

Activity: Debt Checkup

Take a few minutes to answer these questions:

1. Do you currently have any debt? If yes, what type (e.g., credit card, student loan, personal loan)?
2. What is your total debt amount?
3. What's the interest rate on your debt?
4. How much can you afford to pay toward your debt each month?

Next Step

Create a plan to tackle your debt using the Snowball or Avalanche

Method. Write down your top priority and set a timeline to pay it off.

Common Debt Myths

1. **Myth**: All debt is bad.
    - **Truth**: Some debt, like a mortgage, can help you build wealth over time.
2. **Myth**: It's better to pay the minimum and keep extra cash for other things.
    - **Truth**: Paying only the minimum means you'll pay much more in interest over time.

What's Next

Debt doesn't have to control your life. With a solid plan and some discipline, you can take control of it instead. In **Chapter 4: Saving Is the New Cool**, we'll talk about building an emergency fund, saving for your goals, and using savings as a safety net.

#4: SAVING IS THE NEW COOL

Saving money isn't just about being prepared for emergencies (though that's super important). It's also about giving yourself the freedom to do what you want—whether it's traveling, starting a business, or buying something big like a car.

Think About This

Imagine you get an unexpected $1,000 expense (a car repair, medical bill, or surprise trip for a wedding).

- If you have savings, no problem! You pay and move on.
- If you don't, you're scrambling for a loan, using a credit card, or borrowing from friends—stressful, right?

Savings are like a safety net that catches you when life throws curveballs.

Where Should You Save?

Not all savings are the same. Here's a breakdown of where to park your money:

1. **Emergency Fund**
    - Purpose: Cover unexpected expenses like car repairs or medical bills.
    - Goal: Save at least 3–6 months' worth of living expenses. Start small—$500 is a great first milestone.
2. **Short-Term Savings**
    - Purpose: For things you want in the next 1–2 years (vacations, new gadgets, holiday gifts).

- Where: A regular savings account.

3. **Long-Term Savings**
    - Purpose: Big goals like buying a house, starting a business, or retirement.
    - Where: High-yield savings accounts or investment accounts (more on investing in Chapter 6).

Pro Tip

Look for **high-yield savings accounts** that offer better interest rates than regular ones. Your money grows faster while staying safe.

The Power of Starting Small

Don't think you need to save huge amounts to make a difference. Small, consistent saving adds up over time thanks to the magic of **compound interest**—interest that earns interest on itself.

If you save $50 a month in an account with 5% interest, after 10 years, you'll have about $7,764. That's nearly $1,764 in free money just from interest!

How to Save Money Without Feeling Deprived

1. **Automate Your Savings**
    - Set up automatic transfers from your checking account to your savings. Treat it like a bill you pay to yourself.
2. **Cut Back on Small Expenses**
    - Bring your own coffee ($3/day saved = $90/month).
    - Cancel subscriptions you don't use (average savings: $10–$20/month).
3. **Challenge Yourself**
    - Try a **No-Spend Week**: Only spend on

> essentials for one week. Put the money you save into your savings account.
> - Do the **$5 Challenge**: Save every $5 bill you get—watch it add up fast!

Set a Saving Goal

Write down one saving goal and break it into smaller, achievable steps.

- **Goal**: Save $500 for an emergency fund in 6 months.
- **Plan**: Save $20 a week by bringing lunch to work/school instead of eating out.

Keep track of your progress with a visual tracker—like a bar graph or a jar you can fill in.

When to Use Your Savings

Having savings is awesome, but it's just as important to know when (and when not) to touch them.

1. **Emergency Fund**
   - Use for true emergencies (not for a new pair of sneakers!).
   - Replenish it ASAP if you dip into it.
2. **Short-Term Savings**
   - Use this guilt-free for planned expenses like vacations or gifts.
3. **Long-Term Savings**
   - These should stay untouched unless they're specifically for a big goal.

Common Saving Mistakes to Avoid

1. **Not Saving at All**

- Even $5 a week is better than nothing. It's the habit that counts.
2. **Keeping All Savings in Checking Accounts**
    - It's too easy to spend! Keep savings separate so you're not tempted.
3. **Waiting for the "Perfect Time"**
    - There's no perfect time. Start now, even if it's small.

Pro Tip:

Keep your savings in High Interest Savings account and gradually learn about investing options like Stocks, Bonds, Mutual Funds etc

What's Next

Now that you've started building your savings, it's time to talk about **earning more money** in **Chapter 5: Getting Paid Like a Pro**. We'll explore side hustles, paychecks, and ways to boost your income without working more hours.

#5: GETTING PAID LIKE A PRO

Saving and budgeting are essential, but let's face it—earning more money can make life a lot easier. The good news? You don't need to wait for a promotion or a miracle to boost your income. With some creativity and effort, you can start earning more right now.

Side Hustles for Everyone

Side hustles are a great way to add extra income without quitting your main job or taking on too much risk. Here are a few ideas:

1. **Freelancing**
    - If you have a skill like graphic design, writing, coding, or video editing, platforms like Upwork, Fiverr, or Toptal can connect you with clients.
2. **Tutoring**
    - If you're good at a subject, consider tutoring high school or college students. You can even teach online through sites like Wyzant or Varsity Tutors.
3. **Selling Online**
    - Got old clothes, electronics, or books? Sell them on platforms like eBay, Poshmark, or Facebook Marketplace.
4. **Gig Economy Jobs**
    - Try flexible options like Uber, DoorDash, or TaskRabbit.

5. **Turn Hobbies Into Cash**
    - Love crafting? Sell your creations on Etsy.
    - Good with photography? Offer services for events or sell your photos online.

Understanding Paychecks

When you start earning, it's important to know where your money goes. Here's a quick breakdown of a typical paycheck:

1. **Gross Pay**
    - This is the total amount you earn before anything is taken out.
2. **Deductions**
    - Taxes: Federal, state, and local taxes are deducted from your paycheck.
    - Benefits: If you have health insurance or a retirement plan, those costs come out too.
3. **Net Pay**
    - This is the amount you take home. It's what you actually have to work with for budgeting and saving.

Pro Tip

Review your pay stub to make sure everything is correct. Mistakes happen, and it's your responsibility to catch them.

Negotiating Your Pay

Most people don't think about negotiating their salary, but it's one of the easiest ways to increase your income.

1. **Do Your Research**
    - Look up average salaries for your role and experience level on sites like Glassdoor or

PayScale.

2. **Practice Your Pitch**
   - Highlight your accomplishments and how they've added value to your employer.

3. **Be Confident, Not Aggressive**
   - A simple phrase like, "Based on my performance and market research, I'd like to discuss adjusting my salary to better align with my role's value" can work wonders.

Passive Income Explained

Passive income is money you earn with minimal effort after the initial setup. It's like getting paid while you sleep! Here are a few beginner-friendly options:

1. **Start a Blog or YouTube Channel**
   - Share your knowledge or hobbies and earn through ads, sponsorships, or affiliate marketing.

2. **Rent Out What You Own**
   - Have an extra room? Rent it on Airbnb.
   - Got a car? Rent it out through Turo.

3. **Invest for Dividends**
   - Some stocks pay dividends, which are small payments just for owning them. We'll cover this more in Chapter 6.

Plan Your Income Boost

Write down atleast one side gig you could start earning extra money:

- **Example 1**: Offer tutoring for math at $20/hour for 5

hours a week = $100/week.
- **Example 2**: Sell old clothes online and earn $150 in one month.
- **Example 3**: Start a blog and aim to earn $50/month after three months.

Quick Wins to Boost Your Income

1. **Sell Unused Stuff**
   - Go through your closet, garage, or storage and sell items you don't need.
2. **Cash In on Rewards**
   - Use cashback apps like Rakuten or Ibotta for purchases you're already making.
3. **Ask for a Raise**
   - If you've been at your job for a while and have a good performance record, it might be time to ask.

Common Income Mistakes to Avoid

1. **Spending Every Dollar You Earn**
   - More income doesn't mean you should spend more. Save or invest the extra.
2. **Taking on Too Much**
   - Avoid side hustles that leave you exhausted or stressed. Balance is key.
3. **Ignoring Taxes**
   - If you're freelancing or side hustling, set aside 20–30% of your earnings for taxes.

What's Next

Now that you know how to boost your income, it's time to dive into **Chapter 6: Investing Basics for Beginners**. Make your money work for you and grow over time.

#6: INVESTING BASICS FOR BEGINNERS

Investing is putting your money to work to grow over time. Think of it as planting a seed that, with the right care, grows into a tree. Instead of just saving money in a bank account, investing allows your money to earn more money.

Key Difference

- **Saving**: Stashing your money safely (e.g., in a savings account).
- **Investing**: Taking calculated risks to grow your money (e.g., buying stocks or bonds).

Imagine you save $1,000 in a savings account earning 1% interest. In 10 years, you'll have about $1,105. But if you invest the same $1,000 in a stock market index fund with an average return of 7%, you'll have about $1,967. That's nearly double the growth!

Why Start Investing Now?

The earlier you start, the more time your money has to grow thanks to **compound interest**—where your earnings also start earning.

- **Person A** starts investing $100/month at age 20 and stops at age 30 (10 years).
- **Person B** starts investing $100/month at age 30 and continues until age 60 (30 years).

Even though Person B invests longer, Person A ends up with more money because they started earlier!

Types of Investments

Here are some common investment options for beginners:

1. **Stocks**
    - Ownership in a company. When the company does well, your stock value goes up.
2. **Bonds**
    - Loans you give to companies or governments. They pay you back with interest.
3. **Mutual Funds**
    - A mix of stocks and bonds managed by professionals.
4. **Exchange-Traded Funds (ETFs)**
    - Similar to mutual funds but traded like stocks. Often less expensive and great for beginners.
5. **Cryptocurrency**
    - Digital currency like Bitcoin. High risk, high reward. Only invest what you can afford to lose.

How to Get Started with Investing

1. **Set Your Goals**
    - Short-term (1–5 years): Stick to safer investments like bonds or high-yield savings accounts.
    - Long-term (5+ years): Look at stocks, ETFs, or mutual funds.
2. **Choose an Investment Account**
    - **Brokerage Account**: Great for general investing. Popular options include Fidelity, Robinhood, or Vanguard.
    - **Retirement Account**: Like a 401(k) or IRA, designed to grow your money for retirement (with tax benefits!).

3. **Start Small**
    - You don't need thousands of dollars to start. Many platforms let you invest with as little as $5 or $10.
4. **Diversify Your Portfolio**
    - Don't put all your money into one stock or investment. Spread it out to reduce risk.

How Much Should You Invest?

A good rule of thumb is to aim to invest 15–20% of your income if possible. If that feels overwhelming, start with what you can afford—even $50/month adds up over time.

If you earn $2,000/month:

- Set aside $200–$300 for investing.
- Allocate it across different investments (e.g., 60% stocks, 30% bonds, 10% savings).

Risks and Rewards

Investing comes with risks, but understanding them can help you make smarter choices:

- **Higher Risk = Higher Potential Reward**: Stocks can grow fast but are more volatile.
- **Lower Risk = Lower Potential Reward**: Bonds and savings accounts are safer but grow slower.

Pro Tip

Never invest money you might need in the next 3–5 years. Investments can go up and down in the short term.

Your First Investment Plan

Write down your answers to these questions:

1. How much money can you set aside for investing?
2. What's your investment goal (short-term or long-term)?
3. Which type of investment appeals to you most (e.g., stocks, ETFs, mutual funds)?

Next Step

Open an investment account and make your first investment. Start small and track your progress.

Common Investment Mistakes to Avoid

1. **Trying to Time the Market**
    - No one knows when prices will rise or fall. Focus on long-term growth.
2. **Investing Without Research**
    - Understand what you're investing in before putting in money.
3. **Ignoring Fees**
    - Check for account or trading fees. Even small fees can eat into your profits over time.

What's Next

Now that you know the basics of investing, you're ready to make your money work for you. In **Chapter 7: Spending Wisely**, we'll explore how to manage your spending so you can save more and enjoy life without feeling broke.

❖ ❖ ❖

#7: SPENDING WISELY

Spending money isn't the enemy—it's how you spend that can make or break your financial goals. The key is finding a balance between enjoying life now and saving for the future.

Imagine you make $2,000 a month.

- If you spend $500 on eating out, $300 on subscriptions, and $700 on random shopping, you might struggle to pay bills or save anything.
- But if you plan ahead, you can still treat yourself while covering essentials and saving for the things that truly matter.

The Psychology of Spending

Our emotions and habits often drive our spending. Understanding why you spend can help you take control.

Common Triggers

- **Impulse Buys**: Those "limited-time offers" or checkout aisle snacks.
- **Retail Therapy**: Buying things to feel better after a bad day.
- **Keeping Up with Friends**: Going out or shopping just to fit in.

How to Fight Back

- Pause and ask yourself: "Do I really need this, or do I just want it right now?"

- Use the **24-Hour Rule**: Wait a day before buying anything over a certain amount.

Needs vs. Wants

It's easy to blur the line between what you need and what you want. Let's break it down:

- **Needs**: Essentials like rent, utilities, groceries, and transportation.
- **Wants**: Things that make life fun, like streaming services, eating out, or the latest gadgets.

Activity

Write down your last five purchases. Label each one as a "Need" or a "Want." Were any of them surprising?

Tips for Spending Wisely

1. **Create a Spending Plan**
   - Set aside a specific amount for fun money each month. Once it's gone, it's gone.
2. **Track Your Spending**
   - Use an app like Mint or PocketGuard to see where your money is going.
3. **Shop Smarter**
   - Use cashback apps like Rakuten or Ibotta.
   - Compare prices online before buying big-ticket items.
4. **Set Priorities**
   - Focus on spending money on experiences or things that bring you lasting happiness.

Quick Wins to Save Money

1. **Cut Unnecessary Subscriptions**

- Look through your subscriptions. Are you using all of them? Cancel the ones you don't need.
2. **Use Discounts and Coupons**
    - Search for promo codes before buying online or use apps like Honey.
3. **Buy Used Instead of New**
    - Look for pre-owned items on Facebook Marketplace, eBay, or thrift stores.
4. **Plan Ahead**
    - Make a shopping list before going to the store to avoid impulse buys.

Spending on Fun Without Feeling Guilty

It's okay to spend on things you love—as long as you plan for it.

If you love concerts, set up a "fun fund" to save for tickets. Knowing the money is already set aside makes it easier to enjoy without regret.

Pro Tip

Think about the "cost per use" of what you buy. A $100 jacket you wear 50 times costs $2 per use, while a $20 trendy shirt you wear once costs $20 per use. Spend on quality, not quantity.

Your Spending Priorities

Write down your top three spending priorities (e.g., travel, eating out, saving for a car). Then look at your current spending—does it align with your priorities? If not, make adjustments.

Common Spending Mistakes to Avoid

1. **Lifestyle Inflation**

- When your income goes up, it's tempting to spend more. Instead, save or invest the extra.
2. **Ignoring Small Purchases**
   - Those $5 coffees and $10 app subscriptions add up over time.
3. **Using Credit for Non-Essentials**
   - If you can't afford it now, don't buy it with credit unless it's an emergency.

What's Next

Spending wisely lets you enjoy life without financial stress. In **Chapter 8: Adulting Essentials**, we'll cover the financial must-haves—like bank accounts, building credit, and understanding taxes—to set you up for long-term success.

#8: ADULTING ESSENTIALS

Adulting isn't just about paying bills and remembering to do laundry. It's about setting up systems that make managing your life (and money) easier. In this chapter, we'll cover the basics you need to feel confident about your finances.

Bank Accounts 101

Types of Bank Accounts You Need

1. **Checking Account**
   - Used for daily transactions like paying bills, withdrawing cash, or shopping.
   - Look for accounts with no monthly fees or minimum balance requirements.

2. **Savings Account**
   - A place to store money for emergencies or short-term goals.
   - Consider a high-yield savings account for better interest rates.

How to Choose a Bank

- Check for hidden fees (e.g., ATM fees, overdraft charges).
- Look for mobile apps with budgeting tools and easy transfers.
- Consider online banks for higher interest rates and

fewer fees.

Building Credit from Scratch

Your credit score is like a financial report card. It shows lenders how responsible you are with money and affects things like getting a car loan, renting an apartment, or even landing certain jobs.

How to Build Credit

1. **Get a Starter Credit Card**
   - Look for a secured credit card or student credit card with no annual fee.
   - Use it for small purchases and pay it off in full each month to avoid interest.

2. **Pay Bills on Time**
   - Late payments hurt your credit score. Set up reminders or automatic payments.

3. **Keep Your Credit Utilization Low**
   - Use less than 30% of your credit limit (e.g., if your limit is $1,000, keep balances under $300).

Pro Tip

Check your credit score for free through apps like Credit Karma or your bank's website.

Understanding Taxes Made Simple

Taxes can seem complicated, but here's what you really need to know:

What Are Taxes?

- Money taken from your earnings to fund government services like roads, schools, and healthcare.

Common Types of Taxes

1. **Income Tax**: Taken from your paycheck.
2. **Sales Tax**: Added to things you buy.
3. **Property Tax**: Paid if you own a home.

Pro Tip

If you're unsure, consult a tax professional. Many offer free or low-cost services for first-time filers.

Adulting Checklist

Use this checklist to ensure you have the basics covered:

1. Open a checking and savings account.
2. Apply for a starter credit card and start building credit.
3. Learn how to file your taxes (or find a professional to help).
4. Get any necessary insurance (health, car, renter's).

Tick off the items you've completed and set a deadline for the ones you haven't.

Common Adulting Mistakes to Avoid

1. **Ignoring Your Credit Score**
   - Your credit score matters more than you think—don't let it drop.
2. **Not Having Insurance**
   - Going without insurance might save money now but can cost a lot more later.
3. **Missing Tax Deadlines**
   - Failing to file on time can lead to penalties.

What's Next

Now that you've got the essentials down, you're ready to tackle life's financial challenges with confidence. Remember, adulting isn't about being perfect—it's about building habits that set you up for success.

CONCLUSION: YOU'VE GOT THIS!

Reflecting on Your Journey

Congratulations! You've taken the time to learn the essentials of personal finance—something most people never get around to. From budgeting to saving, earning, investing, and spending wisely, you now have the tools to take control of your money and, ultimately, your future.

Let's take a quick recap of what you've learned:

1. **Budgeting**: Creating a plan for your money helps you cover your needs, enjoy your wants, and save for your goals.
2. **Debt Management**: Not all debt is bad, but knowing how to manage and prioritize it puts you ahead of the game.
3. **Saving**: Building an emergency fund and saving for goals is your financial safety net.
4. **Earning More**: Side hustles and smarter paychecks can give you the extra cash to achieve your dreams.
5. **Investing**: Making your money work for you is the key to long-term wealth.
6. **Spending Wisely**: It's okay to enjoy life—just do it intentionally and within your means.
7. **Adulting Essentials**: From bank accounts to credit and taxes, you've got the foundations of financial adulthood covered.

Your Next Steps

Knowledge is power, but action is everything. Here's how to keep moving forward:

- **Start Small**: Implement one thing from each chapter. Set up a budget, start saving $20 a week, or open a beginner investment account.
- **Stay Consistent**: Building good habits takes time. Celebrate small wins along the way.
- **Keep Learning**: Personal finance is a lifelong journey. Read books, watch videos, and stay curious.

Pro Tip

Review your financial goals every few months to track your progress and make adjustments as needed.

Your Financial Freedom Awaits

Remember, financial independence isn't about being perfect. It's about making choices that align with your values and goals. You're going to make mistakes, and that's okay—every misstep is an opportunity to learn and grow.

Final Thought

Whether you're saving for your dream vacation, paying off debt, or building wealth for the future, the journey starts with a single step. You've already taken that step by reading this book. Now, it's time to go out there and build the life you want.

BONUS SECTION 1: MONEY HACKS EVERYONE SHOULD KNOW

Managing money doesn't have to be complicated. Sometimes, it's the small tweaks and creative strategies that make the biggest impact. Here are some money hacks to help you save more, spend smarter, and grow your wealth effortlessly.

1. Automate Everything

Automation makes managing money easy by removing human error and temptation from the equation.

- **Automate Your Savings**
    - Set up an automatic transfer from your checking account to your savings account each payday. Even $20 per paycheck adds up.
    - Example: If you save $50 biweekly, you'll have $1,300 in a year without even thinking about it.
- **Automate Bill Payments**
    - Use autopay for utilities, loans, and credit cards to avoid late fees and maintain a good credit score.
    - Pro Tip: Schedule payments a few days before the due date to account for bank processing times.

2. Embrace Cashback and Rewards

Get rewarded for spending on things you already buy.

- **Use Cashback Apps**
    - Apps like **Rakuten**, **Ibotta**, and **Fetch Rewards** offer cashback on everyday purchases like groceries and online shopping.
    - Example: Buy groceries through an app offering 5% cashback. If you spend $100, you'll earn $5—a small amount, but it adds up over time.
- **Maximize Credit Card Rewards**
    - Choose a credit card that matches your spending habits. For example:
        - Travel enthusiasts: Get a card that offers miles or points for flights.
        - Everyday spenders: Look for cards with cashback on groceries, gas, and dining out.
    - Tip: Always pay off your balance in full each month to avoid interest charges.

3. Look for Free Money

Who doesn't love free money? These simple strategies can help you boost your savings effortlessly.

- **Employer Benefits**
    - Take full advantage of employer-matched retirement contributions. If your employer matches up to 3% of your salary, contribute at least that much—it's essentially free money.
- **Sign-Up Bonuses**
    - Many banks and credit cards offer sign-up bonuses for opening accounts or meeting spending thresholds.
    - Example: Open a credit card that offers a $200 bonus after spending $500 in the first three months.

- **Local Programs and Rebates**
  - Check for utility rebates, student loan forgiveness programs, or state-specific financial incentives.

4. Shop Smarter

Small changes to how you shop can save you hundreds each year.

- **Make a List and Stick to It**
  - Before grocery shopping, create a list to avoid impulse buys.
  - Example: The average person spends 20% more on groceries when shopping without a list.
- **Compare Prices Online**
  - Use tools like **Google Shopping** or **Honey** to find the best deals on big-ticket items.
- **Buy in Bulk**
  - For non-perishable items like cleaning supplies, paper towels, and canned goods, buying in bulk can save money over time.
- **Shop During Sales**
  - Keep track of seasonal sales like Black Friday, back-to-school, and end-of-season clearances for discounts on clothes, electronics, and home goods.

5. Negotiate Everything

You'd be surprised how often you can save money just by asking for a better deal.

- **Utilities and Subscriptions**
  - Call your phone, cable, or internet provider and ask if there are discounts or promotions available.

- Example: "I noticed other providers are offering lower rates. Can you match or beat their prices?"
- **Medical Bills**
  - If you receive a large medical bill, ask for a discount or a payment plan. Many hospitals offer financial assistance programs.
- **At Work**
  - Don't be afraid to negotiate your salary or ask for a raise. Prepare by researching market rates for your role and demonstrating your achievements.

6. Use Budget-Friendly Tools

Leverage technology to streamline your finances.

- **Budgeting Apps**
  - Apps like **YNAB (You Need A Budget)** or **Mint** track your spending and help you stick to a budget.
  - Example: YNAB connects to your bank account and categorizes expenses automatically.
- **Spending Trackers**
  - Use a simple spreadsheet or app to log every dollar you spend for one month. This exercise can reveal patterns and areas where you can cut back.

7. Reevaluate Regular Expenses

Sometimes, the easiest way to save is by cutting what you no longer need.

- **Review Your Subscriptions**
  - Check for streaming services, magazines, or memberships you don't use. Cancel or downgrade plans.

- Tip: Use apps like **Truebill** or **Trim** to identify and cancel unused subscriptions.

- **Downsize Insurance Policies**
    - Call your car or home insurance provider to ask about discounts, bundling, or adjusting your coverage.

- **Energy Efficiency**
    - Save on utilities by switching to energy-efficient bulbs, unplugging devices when not in use, and turning off lights when you leave a room.

8. Make Savings Fun

Turn saving money into a game to stay motivated.

- **The $5 Rule**
    - Save every $5 bill you receive. Over a year, this could add up to hundreds without even noticing.

- **No-Spend Challenge**
    - Try a no-spend day, week, or even month where you only pay for essentials. Channel the money you save into your savings account.

- **Savings Tracker**
    - Use a visual tracker like a coloring chart or app to track progress toward your goals.

Final Word

The key to these hacks isn't just knowing them—it's using them consistently. Start with one or two, and gradually build habits that align with your financial goals. Over time, these small changes can make a big difference in your financial well-being.

BONUS SECTION 2: FINANCIAL FAQS ANSWERED

Everyone has questions about money—especially when starting out. This section tackles some of the most common questions beginners have and provides simple, actionable answers.

1. "How do I start saving when I'm broke?"

Saving money can feel impossible when you're living paycheck to paycheck, but even small steps can lead to big results.

What You Can Do

- **Start Small**: Save $5 or $10 a week. It may not seem like much, but over time, it adds up.
    - Example: Saving $10 a week = $520 a year.
- **Use a Spare Change App**: Apps like **Acorns** round up your purchases and invest the difference. Buy a $2.75 coffee? The app rounds it to $3 and saves $0.25.

Pro Tip

Treat savings like a bill you owe yourself. Automate small transfers into a savings account every payday—even $10.

2. "Should I pay off debt or save first?"

It depends on your situation, but the best approach is usually a mix of both.

Start with an Emergency Fund

- Save $500–$1,000 to cover unexpected expenses. This keeps you from adding more debt when life happens.

Tackle High-Interest Debt

- Pay down debts with high interest rates (like credit cards) first while continuing to save a small amount.

Example Plan
- Income: $500/month.
- Allocate: $50 to savings, $200 to debt payments, and the rest for bills and essentials.

3. "What's the easiest way to start building credit?"

Building credit is crucial for renting apartments, getting loans, and sometimes even landing jobs. Here's how to get started:

Step 1: Open a Credit Card
- Start with a secured credit card or a student credit card. A secured card requires a deposit (e.g., $200), which becomes your credit limit.

Step 2: Use It Responsibly
- Charge small, regular expenses (e.g., $20 for gas) and pay the balance in full each month.

Step 3: Don't Overspend
- Keep your credit utilization below 30% of your limit.
  - Example: If your limit is $500, don't spend more than $150.

4. "How much should I have in an emergency fund?"

An emergency fund is your safety net for unexpected expenses like car repairs or medical bills.

The Rule of Thumb
- Aim for 3–6 months' worth of essential living expenses.
  - Example: If your monthly expenses are $1,000, save $3,000–$6,000.

Start Small
- If saving thousands feels overwhelming, start with a $500–$1,000 goal. This is enough to cover most small emergencies.

5. "What's the best way to start investing?"

Investing doesn't have to be complicated or expensive. Here's how to get started:

Step 1: Set a Goal

- Short-term (1–5 years): Save for a down payment or a trip.
- Long-term (5+ years): Invest for retirement or big future goals.

Step 2: Pick an Account

- Use beginner-friendly platforms like **Robinhood**, **Acorns**, or **Fidelity**.

Step 3: Start Small

- Invest in low-cost index funds or ETFs, which spread your money across many stocks for less risk.
    - Example: The S&P 500 index fund includes shares from 500 major companies, making it a great starting point.

Pro Tip

Invest consistently, even if it's just $50/month. Over time, consistency beats trying to time the market.

6. "What's the easiest way to cut expenses?"

Cutting back doesn't mean giving up everything you love. Start with small changes:

Quick Wins

- **Cancel Unused Subscriptions**: Streaming services, gym memberships, or apps you rarely use.
    - Example: Cancelling two $10 subscriptions saves $240 a year.
- **Cook at Home**: Eating out costs 3–5 times more than

cooking.

Track Your Spending

- Use apps like **Mint** or a simple spreadsheet to see where your money is going. Look for patterns and areas to cut back.

7. "How do I stop overspending?"

Overspending often happens because of emotional triggers or lack of planning.

Practical Tips

- **Use the 24-Hour Rule**: Before buying something non-essential, wait 24 hours to decide if you really need it.
- **Shop with a List**: Whether for groceries or clothes, sticking to a list can prevent impulse buys.

Mindset Shift

Focus on long-term goals. Remind yourself: "Every $10 I don't spend now gets me closer to [your goal]."

8. "What's the difference between a savings account and an investment account?"

Savings Account

- **Purpose**: Short-term savings (e.g., emergency fund, upcoming expenses).
- **Safety**: Very safe but low returns (average interest: 0.01–0.50%).

Investment Account

- **Purpose**: Long-term growth (e.g., retirement, wealth building).
- **Safety**: Higher risk but higher potential returns (average stock market return: ~7% annually).

Example

- Use a savings account for emergencies or vacations.
- Use an investment account to grow wealth over years or decades.

9. "How do I make saving fun?"

Saving money doesn't have to feel like a chore. Here are creative ways to make it enjoyable:

- **The $5 Challenge**: Save every $5 bill you receive. At the end of the year, see how much you've saved.
- **Savings Bingo**: Create a bingo card with different amounts ($5, $10, $20). Save the amount whenever you mark a square.
- **Visual Trackers**: Use a savings jar or a coloring chart to track your progress toward a goal.

10. "How do I stay motivated?"

Money management is a marathon, not a sprint. Keep yourself motivated by:

- **Setting Clear Goals**: Write down your "why." Are you saving for a trip, paying off debt, or building wealth?
- **Tracking Progress**: Celebrate milestones, like saving your first $1,000 or paying off a credit card.
- **Rewarding Yourself**: Treat yourself when you hit a goal—just make sure it's within your budget.

Final Word

The more you know, the better equipped you'll be to make smart financial decisions. Keep asking questions, stay curious, and remember: No question is too small when it comes to your financial future.

Thank You!

Thank you for trusting me to guide you through this process. I hope this book inspires you to take control of your finances and realize your full potential. Remember: You've got this!

www.ingramcontent.com/pod-product-compliance
Lightning Source LLC
Chambersburg PA
CBHW070940220526
45469CB00007B/2467